HEALING AND RESTORING CHILDREN AT RISK

A Training Manual for Counseling Hurting Children

By MK Henderson, MA

HEALING AND RESTORING CHILDREN AT RISK

A TRAINING MANUAL FOR COUNSELING HURTING CHILDREN

Copyright © Dec 2007 by MK Henderson
Published by Brand New Images, Inc. in an Asian dialect (2007)

2019 Published by Brand New Images, Inc. in English

ISBN 978-1-892-555-014

All rights reserved. No portion of this book may be reproduced, stored in a retrieval system, or transmitted in any form or by any means electronic, mechanical, photocopy, recording, scanning, or other means except for brief quotations in critical reviews or articles, without the prior permission of the publisher.

Unless otherwise noted, "Scripture taken from the New King James Version. Copyright © 1982 by Thomas Nelson, Inc. Used by permission. All rights reserved."

Printed in the United States of America 2019

Jesus said, "Let the little children come to me,
and do not forbid them for such is the kingdom of heaven."

Matthew 19:14

Table of Contents

Acknowledgements 7

Introduction: 9

Chapter One: Introduction to Christian Counseling 11

Chapter Two: Basic Foundation for Counseling 17

Chapter Three: Foundations for Healing and Restoration 23

Chapter Four: Spirit Soul Hurts Comfort for the Wounded Spirit 29

Chapter Five: Healing and Restoring Traumatized Children 35

Chapter Six: Providing Proper Discipline: Partnership Model 45

Chapter Seven: Childhood Development—Part 1 57

Chapter Eight: Childhood Development—Part 2 65

Chapter Nine: Therapeutic Parenting—Part 1 73

Chapter Ten: Therapeutic Parenting—Part 2.. 83

Chapter Eleven: When Counseling Fails 89

Summary of Manual 97

About the Author 99

Acknowledgements

A special thank you to Dr. Stan Dekoven, PhD, whom I learned the basics of counseling from; Carole McKelvey, MA (Human Passages), a life saver by demonstrating to me the models of counseling children and her heart for wounded children; Chester and Betsy Kylstra (Restoring the Foundations), for teaching a great series that I had the honor to be a part of and learn how to deal with my own pain and how to help others with their hurts; and last, but not least, Nancy Thomas (Therapeutic Parenting), for your heart for the children in North Central Asia and your eagerness to allow your manual to be used as a part of this training for caregivers with children who witnessed atrocities and were victimized by sex trafficking.

Introduction:

This manual is written as a practical guide to Christian counseling and working with wounded children; especially children who are difficult to manage due to the traumas they have experienced. It is written for anyone who seeks to be God's hand extended to the oppressed and hurting in the world.

The principles taught in this manual are Biblically based and are very practical and easy to apply by anyone who has a heart for caring for children. The practical steps and guidelines of counseling have been taught in group settings at Brand New Images, Inc. "Healing and Restoration" training conferences in Asia, and "Counseling Children at Risk" seminars for children's home directors abroad and caregivers. Because each child is unique, some methods that work well for some children may need to be modified accordingly for others.

MK Henderson, MA

Chapter One: Introduction to Christian Counseling

"Therefore, if anyone is in Christ, he is a new creation; old things have passed away; behold, all things have become new. Now all things are of God, who has reconciled us to Himself through Jesus Christ, and has given us the ministry of reconciliation. That is, that God was in Christ reconciling the world to Himself, not imputing their trespasses to them, and has committed to us the word of reconciliation. Now then, we are ambassadors for Christ, as though God were pleading through us: we implore you on Christ's behalf, be reconciled to God" (2 Cor. 5:17-20).

One does not need to be a psychologist or pastor to counsel. Counseling is similar to discipling. Counselors must understand the fundamental truth in the scriptures above. God sent Jesus into the world to bring sinful man back into a right relationship with Himself. Jesus gave all Christians the same ministry, to bring others into a right relationship with God and each other. In order to love ourselves and love others as ourselves, one must be in right relationship with Christ.

Why counsel? The Bible tells us to care for one another in Eph. 4:16 and Eph. 5:27. Jesus wants a church that is healthy and whole. 2 Corinthians 1:3-4 explains that we are to give comfort and care to others.

From the beginning, pastors have tried to meet the needs of people in areas of healing, nurturing, sustaining, guiding and reconciling. The Bible encourages all Christians to do these things. We are to have the ministry of caring, compassion and, most of all, reconciliation.

Christian counseling offers a way for people to deal with the hurts and traumas of their past. In Phil. 3:13,14, Paul says we should release the past and press forward to reach our goals.

Counselors need to live by Prov. 3:5. "Trust in the Lord with all your heart, and lean not on your own understanding." Direction from the Holy Spirit is needed to guide counselors. Christian counselors need to show the love of God, deal with the whole person and believe that God can bring total healing for spirit, soul, and body when a person is surrendered completely to Jesus. Prov. 11:14 says where there is no counsel, the people fail. Christian counselors help people understand growth and change.

Counselors also need to understand the struggle between flesh and spirit. When a person is surrendered to Jesus, the spirit man is renewed. His spirit communicates with God. The soul—mind, will, and emotions—is unregenerate. The soul is regenerated by the renewing of the mind (Rom. 12:1,2 and Eph. 4). Counseling should be Biblically oriented. We are commanded to love our neighbor and bear one another's burdens.

What does counseling accomplish?
- meets the needs in people's lives.
- gives people a new perspective on their life.
- increases the desire to know God's will and do it.
- deepens the relationship with God.
- restores family relationships.
- heals inner wounds and brokenness of people.
- improves self-image of people.

Basic requirements for Christian counselors are to . . .
- be born again believers.
- be involved in a local church.
- be compassionate as in Mark 1:40.
- ask God for wisdom as in Prov. 3:5,6.

- have some knowledge of the Bible as in 2 Tim. 2:15.
- be non-judgmental.
- be able to keep confidences and not gossip.
- respect self and others.

One should not try to counsel if he or she is struggling with sin issues in his or her own life. For example, if one has committed adultery and has a bad relationship with his or her own spouse, he or she should not be doing marriage counseling.

The goals of counseling are to . . .
- give hope. (1 Cor. 13—faith, hope and love freely given).
- give encouragement to those consumed by worry and anxiety, shame and grief.
- help people grow in the things of God.
- help people see themselves the way God sees them; their potential.
- help people have renewed minds and think in a Godly way as in Rom. 12:2.

In the Old Testament, counselors were called judges. They sat at the gates of the cities (Judg. 2:16 and Prov. 5:21,22). God promised to help the people. (Jer. 17:10-14, Ps. 1:1, Prov. 20:27, and Heb. 5:2).

Questions for review:
- How does Christian counseling differ from other types of counseling?
- What are the main goals of Christian counselors?
- What qualities should one have to be an effective counselor?

When life's needs aren't met, mental anguish begins. When this disrupts family life and relationships, counseling is needed. Biblical counseling should be helpful as long as a person wants to change and rely on Jesus, the Healer. Biblical counseling should not bring shame or embarrassment (John 16:1-3). The Holy Spirit, the Comforter, is promised to help in struggles (Ps. 13, Ps. 133, and John 14).

Here are some difficult questions Christians counselors may face as well as appropriate responses:

- Where was God when this happened to me?
    - Prov. 15:3—He was there; sees all
- Does God really care?
    - 1 Pet. 5:6—Yes, He cares.
- How could a loving God allow this?
    - Deut. 30:15—Freedom of choice.
- Does Jesus understand my feelings?
    - Isa. 53:3—Yes.
- Will I be able to recover?
    - Matt. 19:26—Yes
- How can I be healed?
    - Ps. 18:25—By trusting God.
- Where do I begin to heal?
    - Ps. 34:17,18—Confess your hurts.
- How do I forgive?
    - 1 Thess. 5:24—With the help of God.
- When will I be healed?
    - Eccl. 3:3-8—In time.

NOTES:

Chapter Two: Basic Foundation for Counseling

This chapter lays a general foundation of healing and restoration to build upon in working with traumatized and difficult children. I was first introduced to Christian counseling when I worked as a volunteer counselor/teacher at a Christian non-profit organization that rehabilitated women and children suffering from drug addictions. Many of the women had been paroled to the home and some of the women had supported their drug habit by prostitution. Of course, the children suffered some physical and emotional damage as a result of their mothers' life styles. I spent my free time working with a few of the children.

One of the ladies completing the program had an eight-year-old son who later became my spiritual/adopted son when his birth mother died at the age of twenty-six years. Other families tried to take care of this boy after his mother's death, but he was hostile to them. This was not his normal behavior. He was suffering from grief as well as neglect and trauma from living with a mother who had been using drugs most of his life. He also lived with his father for a few years until he, too, died. Then the boy had no one. My church and I were able to help this boy grow to manhood through spiritual guidance, care, and concern.

Several years later I took an 18-month-old girl who had been born with prescription medications in her system from her birth mother, through the womb. This baby girl became adjusted after we worked with a Christian counselor. In addition to the loss of her birth parents, there was the loss of her grandfather and a favorite pet. Due to so many losses, she had very little trust in adults.

Today, both are doing well. My spiritual son is married and has his own family, a great job, and is a worship leader in his church. I am so proud of him. My daughter has earned a Master's degree and is an over-achiever. I'm also very proud of her. She is well adjusted and can do almost anything she puts her mind to.

Counseling is very important to the development of children because many suffer abuse and live in unstable environments. Abused children carry scars and wounds in their hearts and bodies for years, causing them to be emotionally crippled for life unless someone intervenes on their behalf. We take them to doctors and pray to God to heal their bodies, and we work with counselors to heal their hearts.

To regain the trust of children who have been wounded is difficult to do. Many children have been rejected by their families and hurt by relatives. Each child is different because he has had many different experiences. When a child doesn't trust people, it may be difficult for him to trust God as well. Rejection and suppressed anger are big mountains for these children. They are afraid of experiencing more rejection and find it difficult to submit to adults because of the adults who have hurt them in the past. Only God can bring total healing in a child's life, and Jesus works with you to heal the child.

Most children cannot express what they are feeling, so they act out badly. One needs to encourage the children to talk by asking them, "Why did you do that?"

The child may answer truthfully or he may walk away from you in silence. Do not force the child to talk about his past hurts and abuses. Let him know that you are interested in knowing about his bad experiences as well as the good ones because you want to help him and get to know him. When he feels he can trust you, he will begin to tell you what he has experienced in the past. As he opens up his life to you, ask him how he feels about what he has experienced—is he sad or mad or frightened, etc. Many of these children will be withdrawn.

The extreme form of this condition is called "attachment disorder." This is common in children who have been neglected and abused. We will talk more about this in a later chapter.

Below are some important general practice rules.

- If you are operating a foster home or children's home, do not act as if you own the children unless you have legally adopted them or are in the process of adopting them. If you haven't any intention of making them legally your children, do not make them completely dependent upon you. When they become older, they will need to be independent and to learn how to make it on their own.

- In some countries, children are expected to make it on their own at age 14. More and more children are living on their own in the streets at the age of 8, and even younger. Some have learned to fight and defend themselves and have developed a bully mentality. You do not want them to behave this way in your home, as it would be harmful to other children. Reassure them that they will have plenty of what they need such as food and clothes, etc., and that this behavior is unacceptable.

- Help children to forgive those who have neglected and hurt them. This will take time, and even then, there will be times in the future when their anger will rise up.

- Ask God to help you to have patience with the children. Remember there are also evil powers and principalities at work here as it says in Eph. 6:12, "For we do not wrestle against flesh and blood, but against principalities, against powers, against rulers of darkness of this age, against spiritual hosts of wickedness in high places."

- Ask children for permission to pray for them. If a child does not allow you to pray for him, wait until he is asleep. Then quietly pray over him.

- Quote Bible verses that apply to the children and help them understand God's love and care for them. Do not use the Bible to put fear in a child but to help heal the child.

- Be flexible and allow the Holy Spirit to guide and direct you, showing you what the child can't tell you (2Cor 12:4-11). Ask the Holy Spirit to direct your thoughts and words. Children also need the Holy Spirit in their lives (Acts 1:8, Gal. 5:16).

NOTES:

Chapter Three: Foundations for Healing and Restoration

This next section will explain the foundational areas where people are wounded and need healing. This especially applies to children. These are areas of sins of the fathers that have been passed down to the children. They could have been the result of abuse and spirit/soul hurts causing ungodly beliefs to be formed in the minds of the children. There are negative beliefs children may have about themselves. The sins of the fathers and ungodly beliefs can keep the children from being emotionally healed and whole. It is important that children overcome in both areas to be delivered and healed.

Sins of the Fathers

In a paternalistic society, it is common to have the men rule and the women remain silent. Many girls are sold and used as sex trafficking victims. Women, girls and children have been victimized for many generations. How do they become victims? They are made promises that are broken, lied to, abused physically and sexually, lured into addictions to drugs, neglected, dishonored, and disowned by their families.

Types of sins and their effects that are passed down through the fathers:

- Religious sins—idolatry, witchcraft, chronic illnesses, early deaths, etc.
- Anxiety based sins—isolation, self-pity, rejection
- Deceptions—stealing, false responsibility, cheating, trickery
- Mental problems—confusion, mistrust, mocking, scorn
- Pride—controlling, prejudices against others they consider to have little value

- Rebellion—contempt, defiance, disobedience, disrespect, self-will
- Anger—abandonment, hatred, hostility, resentment, rage
- Violence—abuse, arguing, murder, strife, death
- Depression—sadness, self-pity, suicide
- Trauma—physical and sexual abuse, emotional problems, losses, rape
- Grief—crying, sorrow, sadness, pain, losses
- Shame—self-hatred, embarrassed by what they have suffered or lack

Many have inherited curses from their fathers from several generations back; many years ago. Pray for God to break these generational curses and remove their effects from the children. Forgive their ancestors for their sins. This is spiritual warfare, so we must go by the leading of the Holy Spirit when doing this. There will be more teaching on this in the section on demonic oppression.

Ungodly Beliefs

Satan comes to steal, kill, and destroy our lives, causing terrible things to happen to us and instilling in us the wrong beliefs about ourselves. We also develop negative beliefs about the one true God, the Creator of heaven and earth. What are some of the ungodly beliefs that we may have in our lives?

- **Rejection and a feeling of not belonging**

    In some countries, girls are not valued and are put out of the home because parents can't afford to feed and clothe them. Meanwhile, their brothers are loved, valued, and treated with respect. Many times, boys are put out on the streets to beg, too. If their mothers are sex trafficking victims, they cannot feed and clothe their children.

- **Unworthiness, guilt, and shame**
    When a child has nothing and has been severely used in sex tourism, he will feel shame and a sense of not being worth anything. Because of this, a child may feel a need to do things to gain self-worth or have any value in the eyes of others.

- **A need to always be in control to avoid hurt**
    Some children exert or force control over younger or weaker ones. They may also try to control adults because of a fear that they will be hurt.

- **A physical appearance**—not pleasant to the eye
    Some children have been maimed and scarred. They feel poorly about their appearance.

- **A constant feeling of anger, sadness or depression**
    They must understand that this doesn't have to be a permanent feeling because the Bible says that joy will come one day, in the morning (Ps. 30:5).

- **A girl's desire to be a boy**
    This happens because girls are many times treated worse than boys. They must understand that God has a plan for girls, too. God made each one uniquely designed for HIS glory and honor (Ps. 139:14).

- **A belief that abuse is normal and we will always be hurt by others**
    Many live in fear of being hurt by others again and again (Ps.27:1).

All of the above ungodly beliefs are false. That is why they are ungodly and not truly what God believes about us! The children must understand that you only see good in them and that you believe the best about them. Most importantly, you must relate to them how much God loves them.

How do we overcome these beliefs about others and ourselves? How do we help the children overcome these beliefs about themselves?

First, express what you believe about yourself or others in each category or area that is above.
These beliefs affect the behavior of a child because they are the basis of what they think of themselves and what they believe that God thinks of them. The beliefs are based on their experiences with other people. For example, when a child has a bad experience like rape, the experience forms a new negative belief (maybe that all adults want to rape him or her). This belief causes an expectation within the child's mind. This expectation causes the child to behave in such a way as to try to keep more bad experiences from happening to him or her.

Second: Discover what the Bible says about us in each of these areas of our lives. Write what the Bible says about the child based on his or her situation, feelings, and behaviors (below).
- Rejection and a feeling of not belonging (Prov. 18:24, Heb. 13:5)
- Unworthiness, guilt and shame (Heb. 4:13-16, Romans 8:1)
- Need to do things to have value (Rom. 8:14-17, Eph. 2:8,9)
- Must be in control to avoid hurt (John 14:13-16,27)
- Feels ugly in physical appearance (Song of Solomon 2:14)
- Will always be angry, sad or depressed (Ps. 30:5, 16:11, 55:18)
- Wishing she was born a boy (Ps. 139:14, Jer. 1:5)
- Abuse is normal and we will always be hurt by others (Isa. 41:1,3,4)

Third: Say a prayer or lead others in a prayer to reject these ungodly beliefs that do not agree with God's Word, the Bible. Ask God to forgive you for having and holding onto those ungodly beliefs. Say a prayer and accept the beliefs that agree with God's Word, the Bible. Ask God to give you His mind.

> "Who has known the mind of the Lord that he may instruct him? But we have the mind of Christ."
> 1 Cor. 2:16

Ungodly beliefs are at the center of deep hurts that children have experienced. Ungodly beliefs and actions of others brought pain into the lives of children. Some have endured beatings, scalding water burns, rape, etc., but God, through the power of His Holy Spirit, can give hope and healing to children and restore them in every way to be healthy and whole emotionally!

NOTES:

Chapter Four: Spirit Soul Hurts
Comfort for the Wounded Spirit

"The spirit of a man will sustain him in sickness, but who can bear a broken spirit?"
Prov. 18:14

When Jacob thought Joseph had been torn apart by a wild beast he refused to be comforted (Gen. 37:35). Wounded ones need to receive God's comfort.

God has a healing remedy for the wounded spirit. It is found in Jesus' words. "The Spirit of the Lord is upon me because He has anointed me to . . . send forth deliverance to those who are oppressed . . . who are downtrodden, bruised, crushed and broken down by calamity" (Luke 4:18 Amplified Bible).

Jesus came with deliverance and healing . . . for all. That means healing of diseases and inner wounds. This should bring hope to those who are wounded and have spirit/soul hurts (Heb. 6:19). Hopelessness is an enemy of healing (Heb. 11:1). Hope is the first step to healing the wounded spirit.

Rom 15:13 says, "Now, may the God of hope fill you with all joy and peace in believing that ye may abound in hope by the power of the Holy Spirit." Paul prayed for the afflicted that they might be comforted in 2 Thess. 2:16,17: "Now may our Lord Jesus Christ Himself, and our God and Father, who has loved us and given us everlasting consolation and good hope by grace, comfort your hearts and establish you in every good work."

The comfort that comes to the wounded spirit brings inner healing.

What causes a wounded spirit?

By sorrow of heart the spirit is broken. This sorrow may be in grief, despair, heartache, heaviness, hurt, suffering and torment. These effects of a wounded spirit influence the mind and emotions. If one is happy, his face will show it and if one is sorrowful, his face will also show it. Prov. 17:22 shows us that another effect of a wounded spirit is sickness. "A merry heart does good like a medicine, but a broken spirit dries the bones."

A wound is the underlying cause of a wounded spirit. A common wound is **rejection**. Babies need to be loved and accepted from the time of conception. **Words spoken** to the baby in the womb can cause rejection if they are words of hatred.

Betrayal is another wound that causes spirit/soul hurts. In Ps. 41:9, David says, "Even mine own familiar friend in whom I trusted who ate my bread has lifted up his heel against me." Jesus was also betrayed in the Garden by Judas. Betrayal comes from the closest people in one's life. Parents who sell and/or abuse their children have betrayed them.

Abuse is another way the spirit is wounded. The abuser is usually one in authority. Abuse can be verbal or physical. Parents and caregivers should be careful how they speak to children. Prov. 18:21 says that death and life are in the power of the tongue. Children need to hear words of acceptance and Godly counsel, not belittling messages. Eph. 6:4 says provoke not your children to wrath. Heb., 12:6 says to chasten a son; however, one must be careful to discipline in love.

Sexual defilement causes a wounded spirit. Many sexual crimes are committed against children in the home. Sexual crimes leave very deep wounds and cause changes in the children's personalities. Many are filled with shame and fear. Most feel hopeless and believe that abuse like this will continue everywhere they go.

Abandonment also causes wounds to the spirit/soul. Abandonment is a very deep form of rejection. Newborn babies being left in dumpsters or on the streets, etc., have a sense in their spirits when they are abandoned and feel danger. They are quickly seized upon by evil spirits. Jesus protected little ones from rejection and hurt. In Luke 18:15, Jesus said, "Let the little children come to me and do not forbid them." Ps. 27:10 shows us that God takes note of those who are abandoned. "When my father and my mother forsake me, then the Lord will take care of me."

What is the result of all of this? The devil causes many children to believe that God has forsaken them because of all the wounding they have experienced in their lives. In Heb. 13:5, God reassures us that he has not forsaken us. God says he will not leave us. He will comfort us. Comfort is the only cure for a wounded spirit.

What are the symptoms of a wounded spirit?

Those who have a wounded spirit experience a hurt and ache within. The pain never heals. Although time may bring some relief, it is like a tender wound that is easily re-injured by a simple bump or scrape; then the wound becomes fresh and painful all over again. When a child's trust has been repeatedly violated, he develops a closed spirit. Many will not risk accepting authority figures again. This is a serious matter when the heart or spirit is closed to God. Why?

God is the only source of comfort and healing. One cannot receive from God without trusting him. How can one trust God if he doesn't trust authority figures? A wounded soul may long for death. The devil may cause one to desire death. That is why many with wounded spirits try drugs, etc.—things that lead to death and destruction of their bodies. They see it as the escape from a life which is very painful every day.

Jer. 31:15-17 shows the example of Rachel, who refused to be comforted. She had no hope and her spirit was broken. In Jer. 29:11, it says there is hope in your future. In Ps. 77:2, David says his soul refused to be comforted. Refusing to be comforted is a choice according to your will, a mindset. Hope and faith must arise in order to be able to receive comfort. When one allows God's comfort, he can arise above his past. The source of comfort is God the Father, His Son Jesus and the Holy Spirit. John 14:1-3, John 14:16-18 are promises of God.

How can a wounded spirit receive comfort?

- One must not seek revenge against those who have wounded him or those who are trying to help. In Gen. 27:42, Esau wanted to comfort himself after Jacob robbed him of his birthright. He wanted to kill Jacob. Rom. 12:19 says God will avenge.
- One must not attempt to be comforted through sexual immorality and drugs. Prov. 7:18 speaks of comfort through sexual sin. Sexual sin and drugs do not give lasting comfort. Only Jesus can give lasting comfort. 1 Pet.5:7 says, "Casting all your care upon him for he cares for you."
- Have a forgiving heart and pray as Christ taught us to pray in Matt. 6:12.
- Have hope and faith in God (Prov. 10:28) and be willing to allow him to comfort. God admonished Jeremiah to give up distrust and despair, and God would comfort him. In Jer. 13:19, God challenged Jeremiah's attitude. He wanted him to have faith and hope instead of despair. When you have experienced God's comfort, then you can comfort others (2 Cor. 1:3,4 and Isa. 53:2). Jesus took upon himself all our sorrows so we can be comforted (Matt 27:46). Jesus also

was abandoned and forsaken and knows the pain and sorrow of the wounded. Trauma is very difficult to overcome, but with God's help it can be healed.

NOTES:

Chapter Five: Healing and Restoring Traumatized Children

HEALING and RESTORATION FROM PERSONAL TRAUMA

COMMON REACTIONS TO TRAUMA:

- Feelings of personal worthlessness
- Subtle or open suicide threats
- Excessive drinking or drug abuse
- Withdrawal or refusal to interact
- Deep depression
- Refusal to show emotion
- Anti-social behavior
- Persistent psychosomatic illnesses
- Resistance to counseling or help
- Confusion, crying
- Fatigue, sleep disturbances
- Change in appetite/weight loss or gain
- Low resistance to illnesses
- Frustration, helplessness, despair
- Anger, outrage
- Insecurity, fear
- Anxiety
- Numbness
- Feelings of inadequacy
- Problems concentrating
- Religious confusion
- Flashbacks
- Loss of trust
- Regression, anniversary difficulties

- Work/school/family problems
- Difficulty returning to normal activity
- Feeling overwhelmed
- Irritability
- Bad humor and jokes related to the trauma

Factors that influence one's response to traumatic events:

- Characteristics of the event: type, duration, scope, nature and degree of loss
- Factors related to the individual: health, coping skills, pre-existing stresses, previous traumatic experiences, expectations of others, perception and interpretation of events.
- Social factors: family support system or lack of one, response from friends and co-workers, judicial system, societal views.
- Psychological response to traumatic events; timeline to healing is as follows:
    Traumatic event, survival, disbelief, feelings of rage, self-denial, grief loss, isolation/depression, rebuilding, accepting and accommodating and moving on. It takes different amounts of time for different people to go through these stages. Also, some may go through the stages in a different order.
- Eventually, one must accept what happened and accept that he couldn't have prevented it. One must be able to accept it and go on. Even neglect can be abuse, as children need physical touch, such as a hug or a hand on a shoulder, etc.

Post Traumatic Stress Syndrome is something one must notice in children. Especially:
- nightmares
- flashbacks

- hallucinations
- disassociations (excessive daydreaming)
- avoidance by numbing emotions
- emotional distraction
- hyper-overreaction, easily startled
- outbursts of temper
- sickness
- fears
- eating disorders
- obsessive tendencies

Many times, when trauma and tragedy strike, we want justice. We wonder why the event happened and decide to place blame on someone or something or even ourselves.

When 911 happened in New York and D.C., with so many killed, the public sought someone to blame, the CIA or FBI or someone responsible for allowing this to happen? Who could have prevented this from happening? Some blamed the perpetrators who took over the planes and flew them into the buildings while others lashed out at employers saying they should have protected their husbands, fathers, sisters and brothers.

We often ask God, "Why?" While he may not answer us, we can be content in knowing that he is in control (Heb. 13:5). We can take some comfort in praying to him, instead of blaming him for the event.

God doesn't direct evil toward us. We live in a sinful world and God may allow us to go through trials as a result of the sins of the world (Gen. 5:20, Deut. 34:4, Rom. 8:28). But the hard questions still remain.

Where was God when this happened? (Prov. 15:3). He was there with you. He sees everything.

Why did God allow this to happen to me? God gives humans freedom of choice, even sinners. The person who caused you harm chose to do what he or she did. He had a choice (Deut. 30:15-20).

Rom. 8:28 says all things work together for good to those who love God and are called according to his purpose. So . . . God knew this was going to happen to you and he also will turn it around for good like he did for Joseph and his brothers' in the betrayal and jailhouse experience in the Bible. If God did not spare even his son Jesus Christ from suffering, why would he spare us when he knows the good that will come through it all? God will redeem your suffering and it will not be for nothing!

Restorative justice is ideally what is needed. That means that the perpetrator must make amends to the victim. This rarely happens, but when it does it's a great victory!

How should society respond to wrong doing and how should you respond to wrong doing against you personally?

Ideally, to resolve any type of wrongdoing, three things must happen:
- The wrong or injustice must be acknowledged by the perpetrator.
- Equity needs to be restored.
- Future intentions need to be addressed, such as, "Will the offender do this again?"

Victims need the following:
- Victims need real information and retell.
- Victims need to be able to tell their story and receive public acknowledgement.
- Victims need restitution and vindication; restitution by offenders is important, due to the losses.
- Victims need empowerment and involvement in their cases.

How do you move ahead with your life if none of the above happens in your case?

Remember that God says vengeance is mine. God is the judge in heaven and presides over all. There are no easy answers concerning tragedy and suffering. God is sovereign. God is able to bring meaning into the worst situations involving suffering. God is a just God and when we have done all, we must leave the rest to him.

Although we may feel helpless, through Christ's crucifixion, we see an example of suffering and death. Yet we see victory when he arose on the third day!

Many Christians in foreign countries are suffering for the sake of the gospel. Many are imprisoned on false charges. Others are tortured with beatings, etc., by those trying to force them to renounce Christ. Throughout the Bible, the prophets were persecuted because of their obedience to God (Acts 7:52, Matt. 5:11,12, 1 Cor. 15:9).

Persecution is inevitable because we live in a sinful world that hates God. John 15:8 and Matt 5:10 says that where there is righteousness there is evil. God promises us help and strength through his Holy Spirit (Rom. 8:35-39).

As believers in Christ, we can face persecution with patience and endurance (Rom. 112:12, James 5:7-11). We will become victorious if we persevere. We are not forsaken by God no matter how alone we seem to be (2 Cor. 4:7-10, James 1:2-4). God will reward us as we continue serving him (Heb. 12:1,2; Rev. 14:12, 1 Cor. 15:58). We are called to be committed to God and other believers (1 Pet. 1:5-7). Virtue, knowledge and self-control are developed during times of persecution.

We will receive a crown of life—one like the kind of diadem given to a winner or an athlete in competition in Greece. This is the type of crown we will receive for victory (2 Cor. 5:10). 1 Thess. 2:19 describes another crown, one of righteousness for those who lived righteous lives. 2 Tim. 4:6-8 says the crown of life is awarded to those who have suffered persecution or martyrdom for their faith in God. (James 1:12, Rev. 2:10). There is also a crown of glory for church leaders who have faithfully cared for the sheep. (1 Pet. 5:4).

God rewards those who have persevered (Matt. 5:5, 12, 19:27-30, 25:14-30, Luke 19:12-27

COUNSELING STEPS FOR SPIRIT/SOUL HURTS AND THOSE WHO HAVE BEEN TRAUMATIZED

Step 1: Waiting upon the Lord
Allow the Holy Spirit to be in control of your ministering. Listen for the Holy Spirit to clarify and bring things and bring things to your mind such as addressing hindrances the person may preventing him from receiving healing.

Step 2: Prepare the receiver to receive comfort by the Holy Spirit.
Explain to the receiver what Jesus has done for him on the cross and why he suffered and died for him. If the person has not received Jesus, he needs to repent of his sins and accept Christ.

Step 3: Recognize that the Holy Spirit is within you.
He is the third party who is there to assist and comfort. Try to identify what the person is feeling and validate him. (Show you believe what the person is saying about what happened to him.)

Step 4: Ask the Holy Spirit to reveal hurts and situations that he wants to heal.
>Pray as the Lord leads you to pray as the person reveals hurts and sorrows, etc. Recognize that the spirit of rejection is usually a big factor in the healing of a person and he may fear that revealing things about himself to you may cause you to reject him, too. Reassure him that you will not reject him but will be there to support him.

Step 5: Let the person start at the beginning of his life and tell you his story.
>This is important; especially if he doesn't know where to begin. Pray as the Lord leads you; just stop and pray. The person may need to tell his feelings about what happened to him, feelings of anger, fear, etc. Allow him to do so. If there are abandonment issues, make him aware that God has always had a plan for him, even before he was born! God is able to provide for him even if his parents weren't able to provide for him (Ps. 139:13).

Step 6: Explain to him that God chose for him to be born and to live.
>It is a part of his plan. Listen carefully as he discusses his interactions with other children and adults. He may have been sexually victimized for many years and deeply wounded because of it. Allow the Holy Spirit to work; pray and obey his leading.

Step 7: Realize that God may heal only one issue at a time or several at a time.
>Be sensitive to the Holy Spirit. Usually, what the person brings up is the area that God wants to heal now. Help the person clarify it.

Step 8: Address hindrances to healing such as a refusal to forgive and a desire to seek revenge.

Work with the person to help him release the negative emotions. Some may need to hit something like a punching bag. Others may need to cry and pour out their hearts to the Lord. Ask for Jesus to be present as you listen to him and tell him that God is present. Work together with God until the healing comes and the person feels comforted.

Step 9: The person may not feel comforted immediately, but over time.

It may take several sessions of counseling with the person. Just knowing that you are willing to listen and hear him out and believe him begins the healing process. Only continue as long as you feel the Holy Spirit is directing you to do so.

Step 10: Sometimes there may be demonic hindrances toward the person being healed.

That is usually due to bitterness and a refusal to forgive over a long period of time. Evil is filling a void and causing a stronghold. If you sense this, address it with the person.

PRAYERS FOR SPIRIT/SOUL HURTS AND TRAUMATIZED CHILDREN

The counselor can pray this prayer over a child who has been severely wounded and is full of anger and bitterness. This will help the child release his or her pain.

Warfare Prayer:

"I renounce Satan and all his works in (name's) _____ life. I take his life back from you right now. You will not rob him of the comfort that Jesus has for him. I resist you in the name of Jesus and command you to flee."

The counselor can pray the prayer below for the child; however, when the child is ready, he needs to pray this prayer for himself, repeating the words as you say them.

Prayer for receiving comfort and healing:

"Heavenly Father, you know my life and all that has happened to me. You know the wounds that I have experienced. You know what others have done to me and the pain they have caused me. I come to you with a forgiving heart. I willingly and completely forgive each person who has caused me pain and sorrow. I also forgive myself for having hatred in my heart toward them.

I repent of all my sins and ask you, Jesus, to forgive me and cleanse me because you shed your blood for my sins when you hung on the cross and died. You also were beaten with many stripes that caused much blood to be shed for my healing. I receive your comfort now and healing of my hurts. Please take away my sorrow and give me peace and joy. I choose to be comforted and I accept your comforting touch, right now, in Jesus' name. Amen."

NOTES:

Chapter Six: Providing Proper Discipline: Partnership Model

Family is very important, whether the traditional unit of mother, father and children or non-traditional unit of single parent or group home for children. When a family is disrupted, the consequences are drastic. The family is the fundamental root of society, the foundation of our community and society.

In South Asia, the family structure is disrupted in many cases due to culture and the low value put on females. In the Himalayan Times newspaper, February 21, 2007, it reported of a woman who had forced to live in a cage for 17 years after giving birth to a girl baby. Her husband's family tortured her and threw her out and when she returned to her maternal family, she was mentally ill. They could not afford to treat her so they also put her in a cage. They were frustrated in not knowing how to deal with her illness. Today, she is still insane and cannot walk due to this mistreatment.

On the other hand, boys are treated like little kings and are rarely disciplined in Asian culture. It is believed that a boy child will take care of the parents in old age and insure they get to heaven when they die. Families usually try to see to it that their boys receive an education. Girls, however, will marry as young as thirteen and live with their husband's family, so instead of a good education, they're taught to work hard, to be a good wife. Girls are disciplined more than boys. Discipline should be given equally and fairly, regardless of the sex of the child. Discipline is:

- To punish or penalize for the sake of helping another become self-disciplined.
- To train or develop by instruction and help one to have self-control.
- To bring under control, to give order and correct.

Heb. 12:7-11 shows us discipline from God's perspective. If you endure chastening, God deals with you as sons, for what son is there whom a father does not chasten? Furthermore, we have had human fathers who corrected us and we paid them respect. Shall we not much more be in subjection to the Heavenly Father? For a few days, they chastened us as seemed best to them for holiness, that we may be partakers in His holiness. No chastening seems to be joyful for the present, but painful; nevertheless, afterwards it yields the peaceable fruit of righteousness to those who have been trained by it (paraphrased NKJV).

One who is chastened or disciplined learns patience. God doesn't want us to be quitters, nor do we want our children to give up easily and stop doing what is right in God's sight.

Children need to learn to obey their parents and caregivers, so that when they reach a certain age, they can have self-discipline and self-control. When a child has learned self-control, then his parents can give him freedom. If children refuse to be disciplined, God will bring the discipline through others, like the police, etc. God's kingdom has authority and laws but is a kingdom of love.

Titus 2:4 says to be devoted to teaching the younger ones.

Children are God's gifts to us, rewards to be counted as blessings and not burdens. We should have the attitude toward those we care for as Christ has for his disciples. Jesus prayed, "They are yours, you gave them to me . . . while I was with them, I protected them and kept them safe" (John 17:6, 9, 12).

Children brought up in the training and instruction of the Lord will be an asset to the kingdom of God (Eph. 6:4). The result will be peace and they will change nations! (Isa. 54).
This chapter is about family relationships and the importance of partnership in discipline. A child has a need. When he expresses

that need, he creates tension and a family member, usually a parent, intervenes. The child then relaxes because his need is met. This is a cycle of safety and trust.

An example of this is a baby crying because he is hungry. Once breastfed, he relaxes.

An example of this in adolescence would be a child having difficulty with his homework and lying to cover up. He may be afraid to speak with the teacher about his homework difficulties. A parent may sense the problem and help the adolescent solve the problem. Together, the student and parent arrive at a solution. Because the adult intervened by meeting the student's need, a partnership is formed. This should reduce tension and increase bonding in the relationship. This partnership is repeated as the child grows older and his needs are met.

Two tools are vital in getting needs met: the tool of discipline and the tool of partnership. Sometimes a child's pattern of getting needs met is disrupted. This results in a tense, needy child, pain of betrayal, alienation and mistrust, feelings of insecurity, and a child who is resistant to discipline and partnering.

Children do not always get their needs met. Most children experience some trauma in life, to different degrees. Some children are difficult to discipline because they want to remain miserable and act out in negative behaviors.

How can one help these children?

Believe that each one is valuable and worthwhile.

Understand that each child has a history of various conditions that may have disrupted his cycle of having needs met and, as a result, made him difficult to parent.

Help the child understand that adults make wrong choices and mistakes, too. This may help the child forgive the one who rejected him, as well as the one who abused him.

Help the child understand that discipline is for her own benefit.

The counselor should be aware of the following conditions that disrupt parenting:

- Prenatal conditions—unwanted pregnancies, improper nutrition, birth trauma, birth defects, physical trauma
- Parenting conditions—neglectful parenting, prolonged separation from caregiver, overly rigid caregivers, parents who favor the lighter skinned daughters over the darker skin ones, making them feel inferior (especially in Nepal and India)
- Traumatic conditions—abuse, neglect, abandonment, illness, accidents
- Losses—alcoholism, death of family member, divorce, adoption, multiple homes

Dealing with Youth in Partnering Discipline

When a young person is acting out, one knows there is a problem and must seek to get to the core issues.

When there has been a disruption of needs being met, the youth may often mask his true feelings and keep a distance from adults; he feels this protects him from pain. Examples of these underlying feelings are, fear, rage, sadness, loss, need to self-parent and negative behavior patterns.

Fear and rage are responses to trust betrayed. Now the child or youth has a *kill* or *be killed* perception of life. Sadness and loss is brought about when the youth feels that any chance of reconciliation is lost. The youth develops a sense of helplessness and hopelessness and feels that he is not worthwhile enough to be cared for or deserving of affection. The youth is afraid to express these feelings as he thinks this would destroy any chance of regaining his relationship with the adult. Loss of trust is manifested in anger and negative behaviors.

Since the partnership model focuses on contributions made by each person, parent and youth, the adult needs to be healthy. He needs to have a clean disposition without any emotional baggage. He needs to be open to new ideas and negotiation. However, this does not mean he should allow the youth to violate his established adult boundaries.

The adult must maintain a sense of self; know her limitations and keep personal issues in check. Not letting the youth overstep the boundaries of the adult is very important. The adult should strive to respond immediately to the needs of the youth, and the youth should also give back. This creates a two-way exchange. The adult should strive for cooperation. All tasks should be done with the age of the youth in mind.

Some Rules for Good Parenting:

- Be honest, and when teaching a lesson, be clear.
- Do not always say, "I told you so . . ."
- Make consequences of negative behaviors real and immediate.
- Avoid using threats. Threats that can't be reinforced ruin your reputation.

Tools of Discipline

Principles developed within a sense of self-awareness as partners and non-partners form within a child or youth a validation that certain ways of living are more effective than others. For example,

a disciplined life leads us closer to God as we learn a basic set of tools to help us solve life's problems. Many of these tools are found in the Bible.

When we teach discipline, we're teaching children and youth how to grow out of suffering. There are six tools that do this in a person's life.

- **Delayed gratification:** "Work first, play later," etc. It is painful to not always get what we want right when we want it. When one can delay the satisfaction of getting something now, it develops self-discipline. A child needs to learn this principle and that he will not die if he doesn't get his wishes instantly. Many youth, especially those who have been wounded, think they will die if they don't get their wishes granted immediately. Children will often manipulate those around them to get their needs met immediately.

- **Acceptance of responsibility:** Many times a person will avoid responsibility and act out in denial. As the "self" develops enough strength to stand the threat of criticism and punishment or rejection, etc., only then will the person accept responsibility. Youth with a history of broken partnerships work hard to avoid the pain that they think will result from accepting responsibility. They have been wounded by parents and others, lacking sufficient strength to risk the pain of rejection or abandonment or even punishment. It is less painful for them to deny the problem or to blame others when things go wrong.

- **Declaring the truth:** Youth must face themselves and the world honestly. Hiding from embarrassment and pain only prolongs living a lie. Youth need to be taught to deal with truth. It is the truth that sets one free. Truth sets one free to be compassionate and accepting toward self and others.

Many youth already have a distorted view of themselves regarding their value and worth as human beings. This distorted image of themselves prevents them from trusting others enough to be honest with them. They focus on defending themselves and do not gain insight into the truth of their REAL selves.

- **Balancing of strengths and weaknesses:** When a person begins to understand all aspects of himself, he can develop a sense of strengths and weaknesses along with an idea of what is good and what is bad. Youth with difficulties do what works for them instead of balancing this with trying new activities.

- **Learning new ideas:** It is important for youth to be open and able to learn lessons. Many times, because they are closed and protected, they can't learn valuable lessons. Those who have a history of unmet needs, rejection, and abuse can become closed and defensive. They cannot risk, so learning is difficult, especially due to all of their emotional baggage.

- **Surrendering:** Youth may try to control everything; therefore, they must learn to surrender to adults. Many have difficulties in this area due to abuse from adults who have *forced* them to surrender to them. So now, the act of surrendering contradicts what they have come to believe about life. They will try *not* to surrender, but manipulate and control everyone around them. They are looking out for number one. They must be able to let go of the past, surrender the pain and joy of the past, and look forward to a better future.

Youth who suffer through many disruptions hold onto anything that works, including hoarding food, manipulating others, being rigid, etc. By doing so, they feel they are in control of their world. Asking them to surrender would be like asking them to stop surviving or to be killed . . . to cease living. Many of these youth see life solely as a struggle for survival.

The tools of discipline, in a nutshell, can be taught by the following methods:

- **Walk the Walk**- Model behavior that you desire the youth to display, so he can internalize the values and attitudes of the adults around him.
- **Talk the Talk**- Talk about the above seven things with the youth to help them better understand their behaviors and feelings.
- **Cause and Effect Behavior**- Good usually brings reward and bad usually brings punishment or correction, as shown by real-life experience.

What Gifts can one offer a struggling youth?

- **Delayed Gratification** – gives the gift of **TRUST**, asking youth to postpone negative behavior to work out a better situation later.

- **Acceptance of Responsibility** – gives the gift of **SAFETY**, helping youth to be honest about her behaviors.

- **Dedication to the Truth** – gives the gift of **INSIGHT**, helps to develop the person's insight so he can realize the truth and consequences of living it.

- **Balance** gives the gift of **PRACTICE**, to experiment with what works best for him in a partnership with the adult.

- **Openness to Learning** gives the gift of **CARING** which we adults must model as we process the struggles of the youth.
- **Surrendering** gives the gift of **COMPASSION** adults must give when dealing with youth and asking them to deal with their losses and get on with their lives.

Gifts of partnering and parenting:

An adult's contribution to a good partnering relationship in the following ways will benefit youth.

Recreate fulfilling the needs of the youth whenever possible and help the youth express their needs in words.
- Give immediate response to meet their needs.
- Assume the youth has needs when acting inappropriately.

Assist the youth in learning to deal with her feelings.
- Permission, as in, "It's okay to be sad, mad and scared."
- Modeling by being honest with your own feelings and helping youth put his feelings into words.
- Support by acknowledging his feelings; i.e., "It's okay to hate cleaning your room, but you still need to do it."
- Push by identifying areas where youth are not expressing feelings by saying, "I think you are mad about cleaning your room and that is why you keep forgetting to do it."

Act as a consultant, not a drill sergeant.
- Give feedback on the choices youth make, both good and bad.
- Offer alternatives and consequences.
    1. Within safe limits, let them struggle and/or fail.
    2. Allow them to own their problems.
    3. Decide what is negotiable and what isn't; then make deals.

Be supportive for the youth's benefit.

- State firmly, "I am for you and will take care of you."
- Identify what is best for the youth.
- Prove that you can and will control him or her when misbehaving.
- Use "I" messages to minimize blaming while allowing a choice and help them to see how their actions affect others. Active listening is good.
- Assist an out-of-control youth to gain insight into his feelings and or behavior.
- For every time one confronts, provide support. The support must be nurturing and warm so the relationship itself is enforced.

Remember, the greater the problem behavior, the closer the child or youth needs to be to you. Reel them in . . .

- "I see you are having a difficult time, and I want to help you."
- Sitting just five minutes with the youth gives time to process feelings.
- Restrictions should be related to the problem and for a specific time period.

Within limits, use natural consequences. Allow youth to suffer or enjoy what life dishes out to teach and discipline. The use of natural or logical consequences leads to effective cause and effect thinking. For example:

- "If you don't wear your coat, you will get cold."
- If you waste your money, you won't have any when you need it."
- If you hurt your friends, you won't have any friends."
- If you do not study, you will not get good grades."

Using natural consequences allow youth to do what he chooses and have the consequences without your interference in the results.

> The above is a brief summary of "The Partnership Model of Discipline" by Human Passages, Littleton, Co.

NOTES:

Chapter Seven: Childhood Development—Part 1

Why study childhood development? One reason is to help children grow and another is to prepare to be a caregiver to children.

Understanding child development helps children grow and develop when parents and caregivers are prepared to better deal with various behaviors and situations of children. Children develop in three areas: **psychosocial, physical, and cognitive.**

Psychosocial development is the area of child development that deals with feelings, self-concept and interactions within a broad social context.

Physical development is dealing with growth patterns, coordination and body image.

Cognitive development deals with thinking, problem solving, intelligence and language.

Children are to develop in all three, areas although they develop at different rates. Now we will look at the various age groups and how they develop.

First, let's look at the psychosocial development of one to three-year-olds.

At this age, one to three-year-olds establish a sense of autonomy and are influenced by their families, social variables and cultural differences. By autonomy, we mean the process of becoming a separate person with a separate will. In cognitive development, children develop language rapidly and are influenced by their environment. At three years of age, children make the transition from infancy to early childhood. Their physical bodies are changing and growing. Children's struggles between fifteen and thirty months are inevitable and healthy.

When young children exert their autonomy by oppositional behavior, they are trying to act as though they have the power and authority of the important adults in their lives. Sometimes children say, "NO" to going to the park or every other alternative. Temper tantrums are more frequent during these months of struggling for their autonomy. The tantrums provide a way to release tension, blotting out the past and future; yet children want the reassurance that they are still loved and that their parents are still strong and in control.

Children also have temperaments or different types of personalities that they are born with. These include:
- Easy temperament – mild, positive mood
- Difficult temperament – slow to adapt, negative mood
- Slow to warm up – low activity level, slow to adapt and negative mood

Transitional objects are important to children, especially when moving from one home to another. A transitional object is a blanket, doll, bear, fabric, etc. The objects are familiar and full of comfort for the child.

The family environment is a great influence on the psychosocial development of the child.

Children tend to attach to parents between 9-11 months of age. Between one and three years old, they show stress when left by a parent, even for a short time. The more time and interaction the parents spend with the child, the more difficult the separation will be for the child.

Child abuse hinders the development of the child. Three things are necessary for child abuse to occur. One, an alienated parent; two, a child in crisis; and three, abusing or neglecting parents, many of whom were victims of abuse as children.

One to three years olds have many conflicts. They desire autonomy and independence, yet want to remain close to the adults. Children this age can cause parents to be frustrated. Children are also greatly affected by violence they observe.

Parents and caregivers must establish authority. Some set too many limits, robbing the children of autonomy. Others don't set any limits, giving the children more autonomy than they need. Love is the foundation for caring for children; however, it may not be enough to meet the challenge.

Thomas Gordon wrote, "Children are worthy of respect, acceptance, and consideration." Parents and caregivers must show children they are understood; active listening is very important.

At this age, peer relationships also influence psychosocial development. Solitary play, alone, takes place the first two years where children only interact with an object or a familiar adult. From two to three years of age, children experience parallel play; children are near each other, but independent. From three to four years, they begin associate play, participating in small groups. After four years of age, they participate in cooperative play-sharing ideas, roles and interacting.

Cultural differences have a great effect on psychosocial development. In many cultures, children have little trust but lots of autonomy. In other cultures, children remain skin to skin with their mothers, riding on their backs. These children are comforted at the first sign of restlessness. In some cultures, children are not praised for doing good; this cuts down on children's autonomy. In some cultures, wealth is measured by what is shared. Shame is used in many cultures as a disciplinary tool; i.e., "What will people say?"

Physical development of one to three-year-olds:

Young children in Eastern third world countries showed faster physical development than those in the Western countries. The close contact with adults is thought to be the reason. The children are breastfed and carried in slings on their mothers' backs. Later, at around two or three-years old, when they are no longer breastfed, they suffer from malnutrition due to low protein in their diets and inadequate vitamins.

As two to three-year-olds become more developed physically, they dress themselves and become more independent. They can do puzzles, eat without help, manage pencils and draw. They develop small muscle groups. With walking and running, they develop large muscle groups: they require adequate space for these activities.

Safety:

Accidents are the leading cause of death for children between one and four years of age. Children are accident prone because they are mobile and walk and climb, reaching for objects. They grasp and open containers that may contain dangerous substances or poison. At this age, they are also curious and eager to gather information through seeing, hearing, touching, talking and smelling. They lack the experience and the ability to predict dangerous situations.

Children must be carefully supervised during their waking hours. Care must be taken to prevent injuries, poisonings and drownings. All dangerous substances should be kept out of the reach of children. Special covers should be put over electrical outlets as electricity can kill.

Children also need to be closely supervised around water—pails, buckets, swimming pools and toilets, rivers and lakes. Many children drown because they are not supervised.

Young children are very active and need a lot of rest. Some need a short afternoon nap. Children should not sleep too long, or it will interfere with their sleeping habits at night.

Cognitive Development ages one to three years:

Cognitive development involves the thinking and problem-solving areas.

Children solve problems by experimenting and through trial and error until their goal is reached. The child learns to anticipate familiar events such as eating times and imitates many behaviors.

At 18 months to two years, children begin working out problems mentally. At age two, children begin thinking logically. Also, at this age, children use mental symbols like "ball," meaning, where is the ball? Children remember these mental symbols and may develop fears of dogs, darkness and other things.

At one year of age, children learn the meaning of words and use multi-word sentences at two and expand their vocabulary at three to four years of age. By the time a child is four, he has learned the basics of his language.

Children's playtime is very important as it involves exploring and changing their environment. Play reflects what other children are learning. Usually, children are self-motivated to play and at other times they play to get rewards. Children also have make believe playtimes or role-playing. For example, acting like they are someone else, usually an adult.

Children also make their own rules when they play. They feel, smell, and touch things when given new toys, etc. Most children are actively, passionately involved in their play and resist distractions. Children incorporate new information in their playtimes. Play prepares young children to read and write. Children learn about friendship and sharing through playing.

Children should not be stuck in front of a television all day as it hinders their mental growth and development. Adults should encourage children to play by providing things for children's imaginations. Adults can show interest in a child's play and understand a child's needs to expand his ideas, etc.

A child's cognitive development is greatly affected by his circumstances and environment. In some homes, there is more adult interaction than others. Some homes are noisy and have a lot of confusion. Too much stimulation affects the child's cognitive development. In these cases, children start blocking out the noise; this, in turn, causes children to miss out on hearing things that are necessary for language development. Development is negatively affected by over-stimulation. Some children that were over-stimulated lagged behind in learning how to talk.

Too little stimulation and adult interaction can also cause slow cognitive development. For example, a child left alone most of the time to play in a room alone, with no adult interaction, may not develop well in his thinking.

NOTES:

Chapter Eight: Childhood Development—Part 2

Psychosocial development of ages four to eight-year-olds:

Four and five-year-olds show an imaginative and playful development. They use toys to recreate past experiences and future roles. They are eager to learn and play with other children, to plan, build, and listen to teachers, and model adult behavior. Children can show a lot of initiative and autonomy and take on tasks just to be active. Children need to see the relationship between decisions and actions and consequences.

Children in this age group have a sense of industry and like to build and dress up dolls, etc. Children develop a sense of inferiority when their projects are viewed as inadequate. Children need sensitive parents and caregivers.

Adults and children should show mutual respect and appreciation. They should do things together, such as play in a park, worship in church, having a common purpose, etc. Family influences are strong in the early school years.

Siblings influence development of each other. Siblings (brothers and sisters) are involved with each other during these years and are interdependent. Children need contact, constancy and permanency in their relationships with others and turn to siblings when parents are not available.

Siblings in South Asia participate throughout their lives in essential activities such as survival and passing down cultural and social values. In these societies responsibilities are shared. These systems encourage sibling cooperation, solidarity and authority of older over younger. Interdependence is emphasized.

Parental care giving and discipline practices influence children's pro-social behavior. Most boys like competition and some separation. Television also has a great influence on this age group, and those under age four. Violent television programs can change a child's behavior to increase aggressiveness and violence. The long-term effects of viewing violent television programs is clearly shown ten years later as the children were more aggressive and violent.

Stress affects the psychosocial development of children. Changes in family environment cause stress. Stress can also be caused by hospitalizations, change in schools, birth of a sibling, divorce, etc. Children try to manage and adapt to the changes. How children do this depends on their age, gender and how they view the situation. The older the child, the more sensitive to the reactions of others around her.

Some children are resilient (able to adjust or recover from high stress). Adults can provide support during stress by accepting the child's temperament, rewarding them with helpfulness and encouraging the child to develop an interest in an activity that can be a source of self-esteem. Children should also be encouraged to reach out to others.

Personal characteristics and friends and family support tend to protect children from the effects of stress. Children who grow up in foster homes may feel high levels of stress and blame themselves.

Experience under the age of eight can have a lasting influence on the child.

Physical development of ages four to eight years old:

Children develop large muscle skills, hopping, skipping and running and jumping at ages four to eight. They also develop small muscle skills by folding paper and doing puzzles and cutting. They like to help with food preparation at this age as well as sewing and arts and crafts. They can draw actual pictures rather than scribbling. At this age, their hand coordination develops after the large muscles are developed. Coloring pictures, writing and using drawing tools help develop eye-hand.

Handicapped children: The psychosocial and physical and cognitive development of handicapped children is affected by their disability if they are deaf, blind, hard of hearing, mentally retarded, emotionally disturbed or speech impaired.

Children with hearing loss may not respond to nearby sounds or voices when their backs are turned. They might not speak clearly or might speak more loudly or softly than usual. They may also have frequent ear infections or have had a head injury.

The following are signs of vision loss in children: squinting, repeatedly rubbing eyes, watery eyes, sensitivity to light, headaches and dizziness. Blind children have trouble developing body images that are positive and finding other ways to explore their surroundings. Children with limited vision need books with large print type or Braille.

Emotionally disturbed children are often difficult to manage. They need structure and playtimes, etc. Symptoms are: hostility, depressions, withdrawal, lack of good relationships. They might become involved in many fights, and cause disruptions in groups.

Children need to develop a positive physical image. Some children are hyperactive and can't stay in one place very long. They also have short attention spans, are impulsive and do not have the ability to wait. You might notice unexpected mood shifts and a frequency in touching objects and people. These children need a low-sugar diet, a less stimulating environment and, possibly, medication. They need a predictable routine without many distractions. The ways adults respond to their behaviors also affect a child's physical self-image.

Sexual abuse is a major problem and affects a child's development. One in four girls below 18 years is a victim of sexual abuse. Boys also may be victims of sexual abuse. Eighty-five per cent of abused children in America were abused by someone they know and trust.

Children depend on adults for food, clothing and housing. They also need love, attention and protection from adults. When children are sexually abused and told not to tell, they learn that the world is full of shameful sex. They feel powerless and believe all adults will betray them. Counselors can help sexually abused children deal with their feelings. Most children don't see a counselor because they live under the burden of silence. Why? They may be dependent upon the abuser, and their safety has been threatened if they tell anyone. They may have been told by the abuser they are bad, so they feel guilty. Some do not have the words to explain the abuse.

Children have been taught to obey adults. this makes them easy prey for abusers. Children need to be told that parts of their bodies are private and they have a right to so "NO" to adults touching private parts. They should be instructed to run and scream if they feel threatened regardless of whom the adult may be. Children should be observed for signs of sexual abuse like anxiety when around certain adults. Counselors can help children speak about abuse by asking questions.

Children need to understand that they are not to blame for sexual abuse and that bad things happen to good people too. Children also need to be assured that they're believed and that it is right to tell about the abuse. They need to know a trusted adult will be with them and give them support.

Parents and other adults can communicate to the child that he or she is accepted. Even attractive children can feel ugly or worthless if parents demean or ignore them.

Children need vision screenings, physical exams and good dental care. Adults need to be sure children bathe often and daily brush their teeth.

Cognitive development for four to eight-year-olds:

Eight-year-olds have the ability to reason logically but four-year-olds do not. Eight-year-olds can mentally work through solutions to solve problems. At this age children have many questions, i.e., where did the moon go? Why is it raining? Children begin to understand cause and effect at this age. They learn to count and do simple math like adding numbers.

Adults should help a child improve and practice his reasoning skills and help him learn to communicate. Children at this age should be encouraged to develop creative and logical abilities.

At this age, children should also develop a sense of right and fair standards and rules and the difference between truthfulness, lying and cheating. By the age of eight, children can produce speech sounds accurately. By six, they learn to make sentences. Adults can help develop a child's speech by responding to the child's talk and allowing children to determine the conversation topics. Children modeling, imitating and responding to adults' storytelling and role playing is good for development.

Language development:

Language development is important in order for children to learn to read well. Hearing discrimination, listening and comprehending, language expression, vocabulary comprehension and context use of language are all parts of language development.

In early childhood, many children learn two languages simultaneously, due to growing up in a family that speaks two languages. Others learn a second language when they are older.

Playtime is important for this age group as they become creative during this age at playtime. Children who play are also better at problem solving. Parents and caregivers should nourish creativity by giving children autonomy and independence in making choices. Don't belittle their efforts; provide strong emotional support. What children learn by mistakes may be as important as what they learn by success. Children should be given choices in what to wear, etc.

Parents can help development by listening to children–a developed talent. Be understanding of their frustrations and provide uninterrupted time with adults. Share your feelings and thoughts to encourage them to do the same. A child's imagination can be stimulated by using questions that cause the child to think. Adults can make positive changes in the lives of young children.

At this age, children should have developed some inner motivations. To be successful at school, children should want to be effective and enjoy learning. Different experiences cause children to explore, investigate and ponder. Children should be rewarded for feeling competent and good about their activities. Verbal praise is great, especially when children succeed with challenging experiences. School success is influenced by social and intellectual competence and motivation and memory.

NOTES:

Chapter Nine: Therapeutic Parenting—Part 1

> "Let the children's first lesson be obedience."
> Ben Franklin

I will now give you some specialized parenting techniques for healing children with behavior problems. These techniques have been used successfully with tough children. Normal parenting techniques such as grounding and taking away privileges may not work with children who have emotional problems.

I have a heart to see children healed and whole. The methods in this section have been used many times with difficult children. A successful child is one who is respectful, responsible and fun to be around in school and at home. This parenting is most effective with young children under the age of twelve, but it also works with teenagers if they have a desire to be healed and whole and are willing to cooperate to make it happen.

The connection with the mother is the bond that becomes traumatized and needs to be healed. Some fathers also bond with children, so by using the term "mom" I mean the primary adult caregiver of the child, male or female.

The *real* mom is the one who guides the child, picks him up when he falls, holds him when he cries and loves him in spite of behavior problems. This may be the adults in the home, or relatives. If you are the adoptive parent, do not make the mistake of calling the birth mother the *real* mom, as it makes you, the adoptive mom, seem like a fake mom to the child.

It must be clear to the child who the *real* mom is. That is the person they will usually vent their anger at. They are like a puppy that is wounded and when someone comes to help, he bites them and mistakes them for the abuser. So does the injured child. A child who has been hurt or abused by one mom will seek vengeance on the next mom. The caregiver is the one the child abuses and manipulates. To heal the heart of a broken child is not easy and takes many months and maybe years.

Many children have lost parents to HIV/AIDS or were just abandoned or sold and are now unattached to any adult. They do not trust and some do not have a conscience. They do not allow people to be in control of them due to lack of trust. Because the child is unattached he does not know how to form a loving bond, nor does he want to feel love for an adult and risk being rejected and hurt again.

Children can be unattached for several reasons: physical abuse, sexual abuse, neglect, and separation from birth parents, severe illness, and several moves without parents. These situations can cause the child to shut down and not love, trust or care. The child feels he must be in control, manipulate and have little conscience. Some of these children also have a deep-seated rage.

When a child's needs are not met, the cycle of needs being met as a response to crying, etc., is broken and the child constantly wants limits but does not abide by the limits an adult sets. Children should know how to obey and understand "no." Many of these children do not abide by these directions or obey.

These children feed on anger and they want to see the adult rage in anger. It makes them feel they are in control. You can view the child as an aggressor or one that needs help. Their ability to trust is broken by someone they trusted. Some children have many bonding breaks, preventing them from trusting you.

Many children who are unattached show the following symptoms:

- Being manipulative
- Avoiding eye contact
- Control problems that worsen as the child gets older. Want their way, and will sneak around to get their way.
- May hurt other children and pets.
- Lying about the obvious
- Impulsiveness. They see and they want and they go after it, even if told "no."
- Sometimes they display abnormal eating patterns, either starving or gorging.
- Rage inside, fascinated with destruction
- Demanding for you, but cute and charming with strangers.

There are twelve parenting techniques that must be used in the order that they are presented. The first six months of using these techniques are the most intense. The child should not be separated from the adult caregiver during this time. Be consistent with the rules and stay focused on the goal, to have a lovable child in the end.

The twelve parenting techniques for difficult children are:

- Take care of yourself.
- Establish respect. The child must learn to respect you.
- Create and maintain a heart to heart connection.
- Set limits and help the child to accept them.
- Teach self-control.
- Give the child responsibility and let him know your expectations.
- Expect the child to pay for or restore what he damages.

- Remove barriers between you and the child, i.e., bad friends.
- Avoid the wrong battles and win against the anger of the child.
- Teach the child to think for himself.
- Help the child to process his feelings.
- Build self-esteem in the child.

Now we will discuss the first six, then the last six in: Therapeutic Parenting Part 2.

1. Take care of yourself first:

That is the number one rule for you. On an airplane, they tell you to put on your oxygen mask first if there is a problem and then put on the children's mask. Why? Because if you don't take care of yourself, you will not be able to help the child. So, take time off once a week to do something you enjoy.

Spend time with God in prayer each day, so you will have the patience and strength to meet the child's needs. It is worth it to hire someone to take care of your child or children one day a week so you are completely removed from the situation and can recharge.

Notice what drains you and try to fix those problems first. If the child is whining, have them take a nap immediately. Do not let the child interrupt you when you are talking. Have them sit for few minutes to practice being patient. Do not allow them to stay up past bedtime. They don't have to go to sleep but can lie in bed quietly.

Eliminate distractions such as television or video games. Some children may try to pit one adult against the other. Be aware of that so you don't disagree about the rules. Set up a lock up area where you put prescription drugs, chemicals, knives, money, baseball bats, jewelry,

2. Establish respect.

Let's take a look at the Bible and see how God dealt with his children, Israel. They break the rules and he punishes them by having them spend forty years in the desert. They complained all the time so he demonstrated a parenting technique. "I'm out of here, so when you want to obey my rules and do things my way, I will be here for you!" The children of Israel learned to "fear" the Father, God. They learned to have respect and "awe" for him. Your child should have respect for you and fear you in a healthy way. The titles of Mom and Dad or Uncle or Auntie are titles of honor. You must claim the title and expect to get the respect you deserve. Why? The Bible says to give you honor in the Ten Commandments. "Thou shalt honor thy father and thy mother?" . . . You also hug the unlovable and have opened your home to a child or children that give back little or nothing in return.

You deserve the respect of eye contact when speaking with anyone, especially children. It is powerful, as it is an expression of love or it can be used as a weapon if you only have eye contact when scolding. If the child does not want to make eye contact, stop your sentence and wait for the child to look up, then go on. When you call the child, he must come and make eye contact when listening to you. The same goes when the child is speaking, he should make eye contact. When you reply, also make eye contact. Your position is also important as they should always be looking up at you,

Children learn from action, not just from verbal instructions. If a child doesn't come when you call him, do not always wait on him. Just go ahead and do what you need to do. The child should hear what you say the first time. The correct response should be, "Yes,

Mom," or "Yes, Dad." Or Uncle or Auntie, etc., and "Yes, Ma'am," or "Yes, Sir," to teachers. When telling a child to do something or not to do something it is unacceptable for the child to ask "Why?" There is no need to defend your stance or decision. Getting in a debate causes the child to challenge your authority. When asking the child to do a chore for the family or themselves, never plead or phrase it in a question. Just tell them to do it.

Establish respect through teaching manners. Walking is done next to an adult not in front of her like they are leading you. When eating at the dinner table they should not talk with food in their mouths, and should ask to leave the table. There should be respect for property like chairs, tables and bed, i.e., not putting their feet up on those things. Do not give the child power over the family or people in the home.

3. Create and Maintain a Heart to Heart Connection:

Children need to give and receive affection. Many times, children do not want affection because of past hurts and abuses. Touch is important and children need hugs to have emotional stability and healing. This is best expressed by hugging them if they allow anyone to touch them. They will become rigid and stiff. You can use smiles to gauge emotional health. Smile and see if you get a smile from the child in return. Try to praise the child for good behavior as much as possible to encourage repetition.

4. Teach Self-Control

Children should learn self-control by sitting quietly a few minutes a day. This is not punishment, but time for the child to get control of herself. This sitting quietly can be done three times a day, depending on the child. A child must obey this time that you have set, even if for only two minutes, so he will learn and make progress in other areas. If the child complains, then the more he complains, the longer he will need to sit. He should sit quietly without talking.

The basic skills such as come, go, sit and stay here should be mastered, according to Dr. Forest Cline, by the time the child is one and a half years of age. If not mastered, then the child will have to master this before he can go on, regardless of his age.

Choices are not given to children until they have shown respect and have allowed the adults to be in control. When they have been consistent in obeying and trusting, then they can have a choice such as milk or juice, etc. You make the choices until they are ready. They have to decide to do it your way or their way. For some, that is a big choice!

Children need a balance of nurture and structure or they won't heal. With too much nurturing, the child feels the mom is easy and tries to manipulate and outsmart the parents. In this way, he gets privileges that he didn't earn and will not heal. With too much structure the child feels the parents are *mean*, *too tough* and *cold*; he won't heal, either.

5. Helping children to set limits:

A child feels safe when a parent is strong enough to be in control. When parents maintain limits, the child can learn to trust. A child will not trust someone he perceives as weaker. If he is out of control, he doesn't believe you are strong enough to control him or to keep him safe. So he takes more control and regresses.

Setting limits is being strong, in control and being respected. Being in control of a child's location and behavior causes less confrontations and more time for your needs. When you set a limit, make sure the child understands that breaking the limits results in consequences. When a child does not challenge the limits and obeys, then he can have more privileges. A difficult child should learn to ask for everything; i.e., "May I go to the bathroom," or "May I get a drink of water?"

Do not always inform the child of special events, but use a need to know basis. Do not inform them when you are planning fun events as some may try to sabotage them. Children should not be permitted to borrow things. Avoid the excuse that they borrowed a stolen item from a friend. Any stolen items should be paid back double.

If a child is caught abusing an animal, he should be kept away from the animal even if the animal has to live elsewhere for a while until the child learns that this type of behavior is bad. Some children misbehave in public and should keep their hands in their pockets or carry some things to keep from picking up things in the stores.

Playtime should be limited and when the child gets out of his boundaries or limits that have been set, then playtime is shortened. The remaining time is spent sitting or working. Freedoms must be earned by being respectful, honest, responsible and being pleasant to be around. Sit down with the children and explain that some things they used to do are now privileges to be earned. They may be angry about this. Let them express their anger, but don't change your limits. Privileges must be earned or they will disobey.

6. Give them your expectations of responsibility:

A child will rise to the level of expectations. It is the parent's job to set the level of expectation. They continue to learn self-control and respect for others. Certain things are the child's responsibility. These are cleaning his room, selecting his clothing, helping with the laundry, doing chores. Chores are expected for the child to heal. Chores should be completed before mealtimes and before playtime at least six days a week so it becomes routine. Children must learn how to help the family by doing chores. As they get older, they graduate to more advanced chores such as washing dishes, cleaning the bathroom, vacuuming floor, scrubbing, etc. Everyone may help do dishes; one may wash, another dry, another puts away. No one leaves the kitchen until everything is finished.

Children can begin doing chores at the age of three. You can teach them to sweep the floor and fold clothes, etc. You first work side by side with them for a few days until they learn the chore. Then they must sit when the chore is finished until the parent comes and checks the job. Checking the job is important as it shows you care about the effort of the child. Make sure the job is done right and if so, now you have the opportunity to praise the child. The child is taught to put in the extra effort to get the job done right.

Doing chores is a good marker to determine where the child is in the healing process. If the child repeatedly forgets to do his chores or does them wrong, he is out of control and rejecting bonding. When a child doesn't want to work, he can sit quietly until ready.

A difficult child shouldn't care for animals or plants or be trusted to cook. He could cause serious damage. However, the he can help do the above tasks. The job is just as important as the child. A problem child is not given any money for doing chores to help the family.

Getting an education is something some children may not want to do. Going to school is a privilege, not a "have to." The child should not be reminded to do his homework. If he doesn't do it, he will face consequences from the teacher. After the evening meal, children should finish their school work.

Giving hugs and pats on the back is helpful, even for teenagers. Children who have been sexually abused will often continue sexual behavior, involving other children. Eliminate the opportunity in your home by not having two children sleep in the same bed or leaving children unsupervised at any time.

NOTES:

Chapter Ten: Therapeutic Parenting—Part 2

Points seven to eleven show you how to build up the children and help them mature properly.

7. Expect the child to pay back for damages:

This does not mean the child has to pay back in money for what he has taken or damaged. One of the ways a child can pay back is by an apology that is sincere. The child needs to ask what he can do to make up for the damage. The payback should always be something that has to do with the child's time. For example, the child would rather be playing but may instead have to work to pay back the damages.

If an older child does something illegal in the home, charges should be pressed and it should not be taken lightly. Parents should back up consequences set by the school for bad behavior, etc. Do not take it personally if the child is disciplined at school for bad behavior. If a child damages or breaks someone else's property, he should do something for that person, such as cleaning his room or doing his laundry, etc. Maybe even doing the chores of another child would be a good payback.

8. Remove barriers between you and the child:

Material things can create barriers between parents and children. Some of these things are time robbers and keep children at a distance from you. They are television, video games, music, etc. The children may use these things to tune you out. They should be put in a locked area and only used when you permit.

Disturbed children may try to damage furniture and other household objects, so try to keep these out of the reach of these children. Don't let children waste toilet paper, shampoo and toothpaste, etc. If they do misuse them, they should pay for them or work to pay for them.

Your children's friends can also become a barrier, as a child will find it easier to talk to others his age than parents. Your child should not separate from family to be with friends.

Special lessons should not be given unless the child asks for them, like music lessons, etc.

9. Avoid the wrong battles:

When children are arguing they should be sent outside for 30 minutes to solve their battles. Do not interfere. If not resolved then let them stay out for another 30 minutes.

Tell the child what to do rather than what not to do; For example, don't say, "Stop blowing bubbles in your milk." Just withhold the straw. Don't take a child out in public if they can't control themselves at home. Going out in public is a privilege and must be earned.

Friends reflect the child's self-image so be careful when criticizing friends. It's better to tell them that their choice of friends lets you know where they are in their healing process.

Hair and clothes are a statement of who your child is . . . his identity. Be careful what battles you choose in this area. If the clothes are not modest, then you must correct them but if it's just a silly style, let it go.

Cleanliness issues are a battle sometimes. A child with a low self-image may not be interested in being clean. Give the child the responsibility and step back and see how he responds. In order to eat at the dinner table, the child is expected to be clean. If the child is under ten you can have him join you as you wash your face and brush your teeth, comb your hair, etc. Set an example that you hope the child will follow.

10. Teach your child to think for himself.

Children must learn to think and make choices for themselves. A child should experience the natural consequences of his actions and thereby begin to think for himself. Parents should not interrupt the process by telling the child to put his coat on or go to bed on time. If the child doesn't learn through natural consequences, he won't be able to think for himself. When a child is demanding action, or complaining or griping, a parent should not reinforce this behavior. Tell the child if he wants something, just ask for it.

Do not lecture or nag the child but tell her in two or three sentences what you want her to do. If a child goes outside without a coat on a cold day, he may get sick and he will be cold. If a child runs away, you can't make him stay. Have another foster home ready for him to be placed in if he habitually runs away. Have some one-on-one time between you and the child, reading or watching a movie, etc., or just sitting talking about the child's feelings about some things.

Do not use punishment with these difficult children as it's not helpful for children who have been abused. Spanking or yelling in rage only causes these children to be angry at the parent as the judge. Consequences are used for these children so they think about their bad behavior. For example, the consequences of wearing white socks in the mud are they get to wash them. Make a list of consequences so you are ready.

Some children need to know everything in order to control. Do not answer all of their questions; just simply tell them they will find out later when it is time for them to know.

11. Guide the processing of feelings.

A disturbed child may have rage that they have kept inside. Help the child process these feelings by locating them, stating what they are and accepting them.

How? By asking "What are you feeling?" Tell them you understand why they feel the way they do. A child's unresolved anger shows up in destruction or violence. Ask the child daily how mad he is, on a scale of one to ten. The rage is usually directed at the mother, especially if the child has been abused, because he feels the mother did not protect him.

A child may be breaking things a lot but is not really clumsy, just full of anger. The parent needs to hold the child and ask the child what happened? Once he tells his story, ask him how he feels about it. If he says he feels mad, ask him how he is handling his mad feelings. When a child is non-compliant, destructive and disrespectful, he is usually angry. The anger covers up all his other emotions. Usually sadness and fear are covered up in anger.

12. Building self-esteem in children:

Self-esteem is the foundation upon which a person's personality is built. Self-esteem is developed by positive feelings being projected by a loved one. Acceptance builds self-esteem and rejection destroys it. Do not bribe the child to do better by saying if you do this . . . then I will do this . . . or I will get you what you want if you will . . .

Rewards and bonuses are fine, but a child must want to do what is right because it is within him to do so. A reward should be a surprise, not something the child tells you to give him.

Other self-image tools that build up a child are: calling her a special name, having photos of the child on display and introducing the child by referring to her talents, also. Try to notice the child doing something right and use positive statements about the child. A child who does not see the parent stronger than herself will not develop a good self-image.

Remember, a child in transition is a child in pain. Moving a child from one family to another causes loss. When a child is moved, great care should be taken to lessen the shock. A grieving child will act out their homesickness rather than talk about it. A child may regress when moved, although it is usually temporary.

If you know anything about the child's birth parents, never talk negatively about them. They're made from the same cloth!

Forgive and forget each day's transgressions. Never let the sun set on anger. End each day with a hug and make it clear that no matter what a child has done, you still love him. Good morning is the start of a new day.

NOTES:

Chapter Eleven: When Counseling Fails

Jesus commanded the church to preach the gospel with signs following. The first sign mentioned is deliverance from evil spirits. Mark 16:15-20 says, "In my name they will cast out demons."

Believers in Christ have spiritual authority to act. Luke 10:1 says, in Jesus words, "I have given you authority to trample on snakes and scorpions—and to overcome all the power of the enemy, nothing will harm you!"

In Luke 9:37-42, a man asked Jesus to take authority over an evil spirit that was affecting his son. In Matthew 15:26 a Gentile woman requested that Jesus deliver her daughter from evil spirits. Jesus told her deliverance was the children's bread. He also told her that she had great faith because she believed Jesus could set her daughter free.

Christians can't be demon-possessed because they have the Holy Spirit living on the inside. But they can be affected by evil spirits and oppressed by them if they allow it. When evil spirits influence Christians, they are trespassing without a legal right. Therefore, they must be subject to the authority of the name of Jesus who has redeemed us by His blood.

How can an evil spirit influence a Christian? I Cor. 6:19 says your body is the temple of the Holy Spirit. The temple in Jerusalem had three parts—the outer court, the Holy Place and the Holy of Holies. The presence of God dwelt in the Holy of Holies. The three compartments in the temple correspond to man's three parts: body, soul, and spirit. A Christian's spirit is like the Holy of Holies where the Holy Spirit dwells. However, the Holy Spirit desires for us to submit our temple to his control. That includes our emotions, mind and will. Jesus threw the money changers out of the outer part of the temple because they were defiling the temple (Matt. 21:12). Evil spirits can break down our wills or self-control. That is the reason some people struggle to do the right thing and continue doing wrong.

Many children have wounds of rejection and abandonment from birth that gave access and opened the door to evil spirits. They need to be free from this demonic oppression. Who can pray for them to be set free? Any pastor or layperson or elder in the church, as well as parents or guardians of the child, can pray for the child to be delivered. He must know his spiritual authority in Christ, and allow the Holy Spirit to direct him.

Where does one begin to command evil spirits to leave children? How do you know what spirits are affecting the child? Whenever you try to minister to the child, certain behaviors usually show themselves. The evil spirits get agitated and start accusing you of not loving the child, etc. For example, many children have a spirit of rejection that will make them believe that no one loves them. A child with a spirit of hatred may tell you he hates you and wants to kill you; he may also have a spirit of murder.

Other evil spirits common in children are—defiance, "Don't tell me what to do;"—self-will, "I will do what I want;"—stubbornness, etc. Many evil spirits affecting children are rooted in rejection and self-pity; others are rooted in bitterness and rebellion.

Many times, children are punished over and over in the flesh for things the evil spirits are doing through them. In this case it seems the punishment isn't working. That means the evil spirits must leave so the child is free to obey and cooperate.

If a group of children have similar bad behaviors and it appears that counseling and discipline aren't working, one can pray the prayer of deliverance over the entire group.

Evil spirits hate the fruit of the Spirit, which is (Gal. 5:22,23) love, joy, peace, patience, gentleness, kindness, goodness, faithfulness, and self-control. One can call out all evil spirits that hate the fruit of the Spirit and tell them to leave in the name of Jesus. You do not have to explain to the children in detail what you are doing. It all depends on the age.

- Birth to two years—hold them and speak gently, praying, "Heavenly Father, I declare that this child is under the covering of the blood of Jesus. This child is in my home and my care. I have authority over him. Satan has no right to this child and I command every tormenting spirit to leave this child now." The child may stop crying or wrestling, etc., and be at peace.

- Three to twelve years – look directly into their eyes and confront the evil spirits declaring your authority in Christ. You can tell the child that his body is the temple of the Holy Spirit and Jesus wants it to be clean so evil spirits can't live there. Only Jesus can live there in his heart. If he hasn't received Jesus, ask him to repent and confess his sins and invite Jesus into his heart. In older children, you are dealing with their wills.

- Thirteen years to adult – the child should be born again and surrender his will to Jesus, repenting of his sins. He needs to forgive those who have hurt him. If he resists, he probably is being affected by a strong-willed spirit of defiance or rebellion. You must demand those spirits to let go of the person.

Jesus always spoke to evil spirits with authority and they obeyed him. We must use the name of Jesus in dealing with evil spirits because it is powerful and the blood of Jesus is something that evil spirits can't stand up under. Command them to remove themselves away from the person by the name of Jesus and by the blood of Jesus. (Rev. 12:10,11). They overcame him by the blood of the lamb. Lay hands on the child to put the power of the Holy Spirit upon the child as you pray this prayer:

"Dear Heavenly Father, this child is covered by the blood of Jesus, so Satan's plans for this child cannot come to pass. All evil spirits inherited and assigned to this child must go now. This child will have peace and fulfill God's plan for his life."

Next, name the evil spirits that have influenced the child as the Holy Spirit brings them to your mind, and command them to go in Jesus' name and by the blood of Jesus. (Matt. 19:13-15). Jesus himself laid hands on the children. Place your hand upon the child's head or shoulder. Some evil spirits will react to your laying on hands and the child will try to remove your hand saying, "That hurt." or "That burns." etc. Just keep your hand there and continue praying and demanding the evil spirit to release his influence on the child now in Jesus' name.

Pray for the child's will to be submitted to God; especially, if he is fighting you. Pray that his will be brought into submission by your authority in Jesus' name. Do not give in to resistance. You are dealing with spirits of rebellion, self-will, defiance, etc. This is a spiritual battle that you need to see through to victory. Never show frustration when dealing with evil spirits but keep calm at all times.

Speak peace to the child. Evil spirits like to stir up frustration and conflict in the home to destroy peace and joy. Put the blame where it belongs, on the work of Satan. As long as the child is struggling, the victory has not been won. Keep speaking in authority, although you don't have to yell or speak loudly. Depend on the Holy Spirit to give you the words.

You are not wrestling with flesh and blood but principalities and powers of darkness (Eph. 6:12). Continue to pressure the evil spirits to go using the name of Jesus—proclaiming the power of Christ's blood. Have the child do something to break his agreement with the evil spirits such as opening his mouth or sitting up, etc. He can also tell the evil spirits to go himself. This strips the evil spirits of their power. The person you are praying for must cooperate. In rare cases, a child may be spanked to stop him from agreeing with the evil spirits. Why? Self-will and stubbornness can keep a child from being set free from evil spirits.

Sometimes when deliverance is difficult, you may have to call out the group of spirits that are working together in the child. This happens often with children who have been labeled problem children. Don't label children, as there is power in your words. (Prov. 18:21) Speak positive words of praise and blessings over the children.

When praying for a group, cover each one with the blood of Jesus and bind every spirit that would try to rob them of what God has for them. Forbid Satan to hinder, distract, confuse or in any way interfere with this time. We take back all that Satan has stolen and has spoiled in this child or group. Invite the Holy Spirit to come and cast out the evil spirits, commanding them to go in Jesus name. The Holy Spirit may reveal to you the names of the evil spirits. Have faith in God that these evil spirits will go, regardless of distractions like laughing and coughing, or spitting up, etc. Once the child is free, lay hands on him and bless him (Mark 10:16).

It is good to have an understanding of evil spirits that are common to children (1 Cor. 14:1). Discern through the Holy Spirit what they are.

Here is a list of evil spirits common to disturbed children.
- Inherited curses (sins of the father)
    Ex. Abraham and Sara, Isaac and Rebekah
- Lying
- Prenatal circumstances
- Conception circumstances
- Birthing traumas, childhood traumas
- Separation from mother after birth causes rejection spirit
- Abuses: sexual and abandonment
- Fears tormenting spirits
- Family turmoil
- Death in family
- Familiar spirits (they see and talk to them)
- Sexual abuse causes the following:
    (Symptoms vary from person to person)
- Fears, insecurity, vulnerability, fear of men, women
- Lust, sexual spirits, homosexuality, promiscuity
- Defilement, unclean, innocence lost
- Guilt shame, self-blame
- Soul ties
- Self-hatred, dual personality
- Trauma, death, loss of family, torture
- Memory blockage

LIVING IN FREEDOM

Now that the child is free from the activities of evil spirits and their oppression in his life, one needs to provide proper discipline for the child to grow physically, emotionally and spiritually and remain free. The purpose of discipline is:
- To punish or penalize for the sake of helping one to have self-discipline.
- To train or develop by instruction and help one to have self-control.
- To bring under control, to give order and correct.

Hebrews 12:7-11 shows us discipline from God's perspective. If you endure chastening, God deals with you as sons. For what son is there whom a father does not chasten? Furthermore, we have had human fathers who corrected us and we paid them respect. Shall we not much more readily be in subjection to the father of spirits and live? Now, no chastening seems to be joyful for the present, but painful; nevertheless, afterwards it yields the peaceable fruit of righteousness to those who have been trained by it. (Re-read Chapter Six on Providing Proper Discipline.)

NOTES:

Summary of Manual

In utilizing this counselor's manual, I hope that you will be able to go to the chapter or section that you need after you have read it from the beginning to the end.

In reading the first chapter I hope that you will be encouraged to know that anyone can counsel children if he has the desire to do so and a heart of compassion. One does not have to be a professional counselor to understand the needs of children and others.

In the second chapter we tell of a very common occurrence in children called "reactive attachment syndrome" or "disorder" that happens when children have been abandoned or rejected or do not know their birth parents due to being separated at birth. It also explains what to do and what not to do for these children. These dos and don'ts are very important to follow when working with these type of children. One can get a lot out of the manual just reading this chapter.

In chapter three we want you to know that many problems a child has may be related to his birth parents and the family problems that the child is predisposed to, causing the child to be disagreeable. This chapter tells how to pray for these children to be free from the curses and ungodly beliefs of their parents.

In chapter four and five we discuss spirit/soul hurts that are common in children and adults and how we can let God heal them. Many children have been wounded and greatly traumatized to the point where their behavior is very abnormal. Many children have been raped or used as sex slaves, etc.

In chapter six we discuss discipline through partnering with the child or adolescent to help him to understand the adults want to help him get better and have a better life. The child learns to accomplish tasks and goals to feel good about himself. He also learns that certain behaviors have consequences so he must make good choices or face the consequences.

In chapter seven we discuss child development and how a child develops physically and cognitively (mind) and emotionally (feelings). We learn how they develop at certain ages and what to expect from each age group in their development.

In chapter eight you will learn parenting techniques for working with difficult children who find it hard to trust and obey adults. It will help you have more patience with these children who probably adjusted to life on the streets and being independent.

Chapter nine is a totally spiritual chapter regarding what to do if you have tried everything in the manual for your children and nothing works! It could be that your child has deep enough wounds and anger and bitterness that demonic forces have become a part of his or her life and are opposing the healing of the child. This chapter tells you the best way to deal with these children, as they usually try your patience and stress you greatly.

We are grateful for people like you who reach out to the unlovely and offer your compassion and care as well as tough love! May God bless you and reward you for taking the time and sacrificing a part of your lives for children at risk.

About the Author

MK Henderson is the founder and director of Brand New Images, Inc. MK has a passion for being a voice for the voiceless, especially children who have no one to speak for them. She has spent nearly a lifetime advocating for and counseling children. MK has worked with child psychologists, child welfare workers, and others in caring for children. She believes in the Biblical mandate to care for the children, especially orphans. MK has been an advocate for children who have been used in sex-trafficking and child labor, victims of severe abuse

This training manual has taken into account the wounded children and how to minister healing and restoration to them in adopted homes, foster homes, and international children's home settings.

The following sources were used in this manual

Attachment Disorder by Carole McKelvey, MA; Human Passages

Comfort for the Wounded Spirit by Frank and Ida Mae Hammond, 1992, The Children's Bread Ministry

Dynamics of Christian Counseling by Stan Dekoven, Phd.

Early Childhood Development by Sandra Anselmoi, 1987 Merrill Publishing (Sections used with author permission)

A Manual for Children's Deliverance by Frank and Ida Mae Hammond, 1996 Impace Christian Books

On Belay, An Introduction to Christian Counseling by Stan DeKoven, Phd.

The Partnership Model of Discipline by Human Passages

Power Counseling in the 21st Century by Stan DeKoven, PhD

Restoring the Foundations by Chester and Betsy Kylstra, 1994, 1996, 2000, Proclaiming His Word Publications (Sections used with author permission)

When Love is Not Enough by Nancy Thomas, 1997, Therapeutic Parenting (Sections used with author permission)

This manual was originally written in Asian languages for use in children's homes and later adapted for English speaking cultures.

For questions or comments regarding this manual or to order print copies, please email: brandnewimagesinc@aol.com.

www.ingramcontent.com/pod-product-compliance
Lightning Source LLC
Chambersburg PA
CBHW071407080526
44587CB00017B/3204